People in the Community

People Who Help Us

Rebecca Rissman

Heinemann Library
Chicago, Illinois

www.capstonepub.com
Visit our website to find out
more information about
Heinemann-Raintree books.

To order:
☎ Phone 800-747-4992
💻 Visit www.capstonepub.com
to browse our catalog and order online.

©2010 Heinemann Library
an imprint of Capstone Global Library, LLC
Chicago, Illinois

Edited by Rebecca Rissman, Siân Smith, and Charlotte Guillain
Designed by Kimberly Miracle and Joanne Malivoire
Picture research by Tracy Cummins and Kim Tidwell
Originated by Capstone Global Library
Printed in the United States of America in Stevens Point,
Wisconsin.   052013   007400CPS

15 14 13
10 9 8 7 6 5 4 3

Library of Congress Cataloging-in-Publication Data
Rissman, Rebecca.
  People Who Help Us / Rebecca Rissman.
    p. cm.
  Includes bibliographical references and index.
  ISBN 978-1-4329-3343-2 (hc) -- ISBN 978-1-4329-3344-9
(pb) 1. Communities--Juvenile literature. 2. Community life-
-Juvenile literature. I. Title.
  HM756.R573 2008
  307--dc22
                            2008055664

Acknowledgments

The author and publishers are grateful to the following for
permission to reproduce copyright material:
Age Fotostock **p. 15 left** (© Jeremy Woodhouse); Alamy **pp.
5 right** (© GoGo Images Corporation), **14 right** (© Nancy G
Fire Photography, Nancy Greifenhagen), **18** (© Ariel Skelley),
19 middle (© Juniors Bildarchiv), **19 right** (© Olaf Doering);
Corbis **p. 21** (© Lucy Nicholson/Reuters); Getty Images **pp. 8
left** (The Image Bank/Yellow Dog Productions Inc.), **8 right**
(Stone/Bruce Foster), **9 right** (Royalty Free), **10** (Somos/
Veer), **11 left** (Mike Powell), **13** (Karin Dreyer), **16 left** (Tom
Stoddart Archive/Hulston Archive), **17 right** (Alexander
Hassenstein/Staff), **22 left** (Karin Dreyer); istockphoto **pp.
6** (© aldomurillo), **12** (© Nathan Gleave); Photolibrary **pp. 4**
(Photodisc/ © Glen Allison), **11 right** (© Thomas Barwick);
Shutterstock **pp. 5 left** (© Mikhail Levit), **7** (© Philip Lange), 9
left (© salamanderman), **14 left** (© Steve Noakes), **15 right** (©
Fiorentini Massimo), **19 left** (© Mark William Penny), **20** (©
Ron Hilton), **22 middle** (© Mark William Penny), **31 right** (©
Steve Noakes).

Cover photograph of a school teacher sitting with pupils in
Sri Lanka reproduced with permission of Getty Images/ ©
Hugh Sitton. Back cover photograph of firemen with a burning
car reproduced with permission of Shutterstock/ © Ron
Hilton.

We would like to thank Nancy Harris and Adriana Scalise for
their help in the preparation of this book.

Every effort has been made to contact copyright holders
of any material reproduced in this book. Any omissions
will be rectified in subsequent printings if notice is given
to the publisher.

Some words are shown in bold, **like this**. They are
explained in "Words to Know" on page 23.

Contents

About this series

Books in the **People in the Community** series introduce readers to what a community is, as well as some common jobs found in communities around the globe. Use this book to stimulate discussion about community helpers and different types of communities.

What Is a Community?

A **community** is a group of people with something in common. A community could be a group of people who live in the same area or who can speak the same language.

A community could be a group of people who have the same religion or who go to the same school. People can be part of lots of different communities at the same time.

Some **communities** are very big. A whole country can be a community. Some communities are small.
A family or a group of friends can be a community.

When people talk about the community, they usually mean a group of people who live in the same area.

Working in the Community

People in the **community** help each other when they work at different jobs. People work to **earn** money. The jobs they do help people in different ways.

goods

services

Some people work by selling **goods**. Goods are things people need to eat or use. Some people work by selling **services**. Services are jobs done for other people.

People Who Help Us Stay Healthy

Doctors help people in the **community** stay healthy. Doctors help when people are sick. Doctors help when people are hurt.

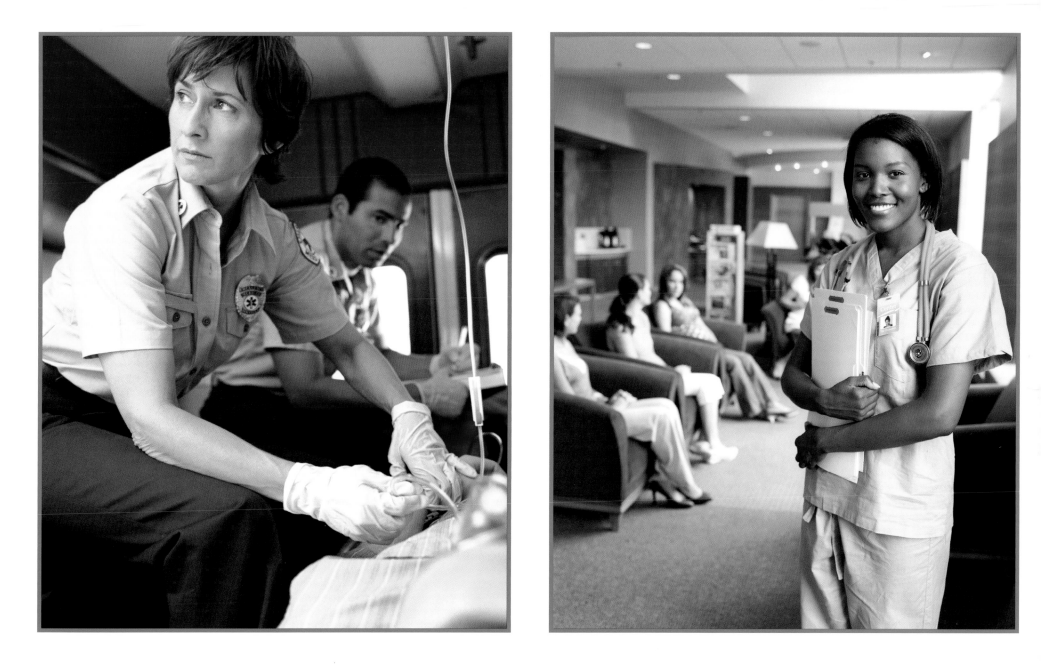

Paramedics work with doctors. Paramedics help **patients** get to the doctor. Nurses work with doctors. Nurses help care for patients.

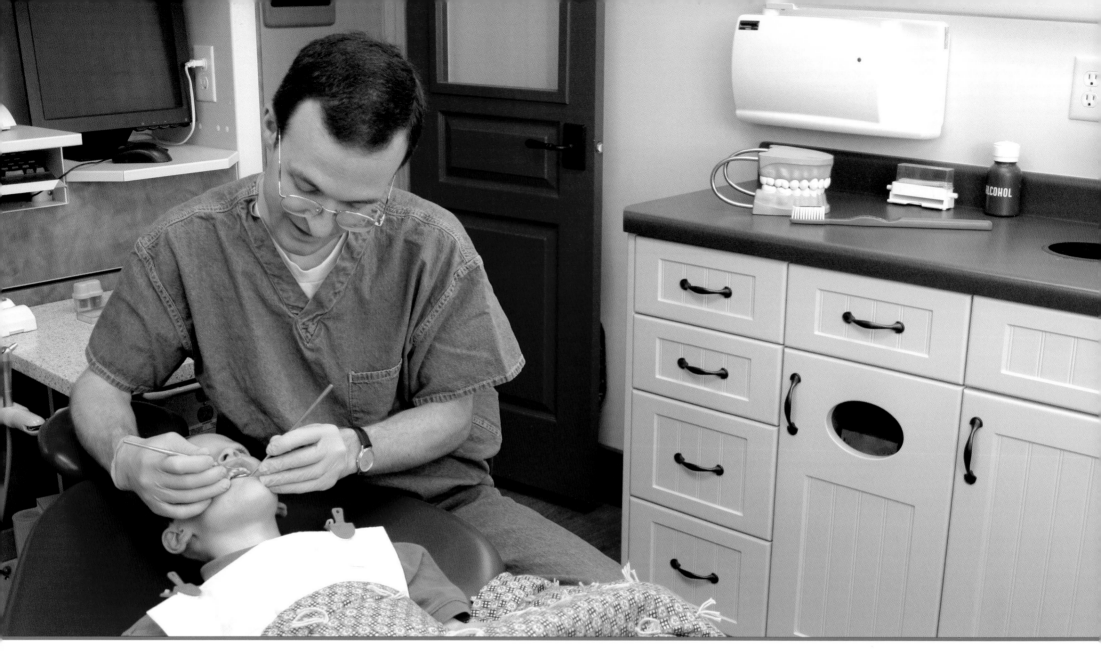

Dentists also help people in the **community** stay healthy. Dentists check people's teeth. Dentists help care for people's teeth.

Hygienists work with dentists. Hygienists help to clean people's teeth. Hygienists show people how to clean their teeth.

People Who Help Us Stay Safe

Firefighters help people in the **community** stay safe. Firefighters put out fires. Firefighters help people to escape from fires.

Police officers help people in the community stay safe. Police officers keep drivers safe. Police officers **arrest** people who break the law. They help fight **crime**.

People Who Help Others Learn

Teachers help people in the **community** to learn.
Teachers teach students many different **subjects**.
Teachers teach **facts** and different **skills**.

Coaches help people in the community to learn.
Coaches teach people how to play different sports.
Coaches help people to stay healthy, too.

People Who Help Animals

Vets help animals to stay healthy. Vets help animals that are sick.

Vets help pets, farm animals, and zoo animals. Vets help the **community** by caring for our animals.

Working Together

All the different jobs people do in the **community** are important. We can do a lot more when we work together than when we work by ourselves.

Helping each other and working together makes life better for everyone.

Community Helpers

How do the people in these pictures help
their **community**?

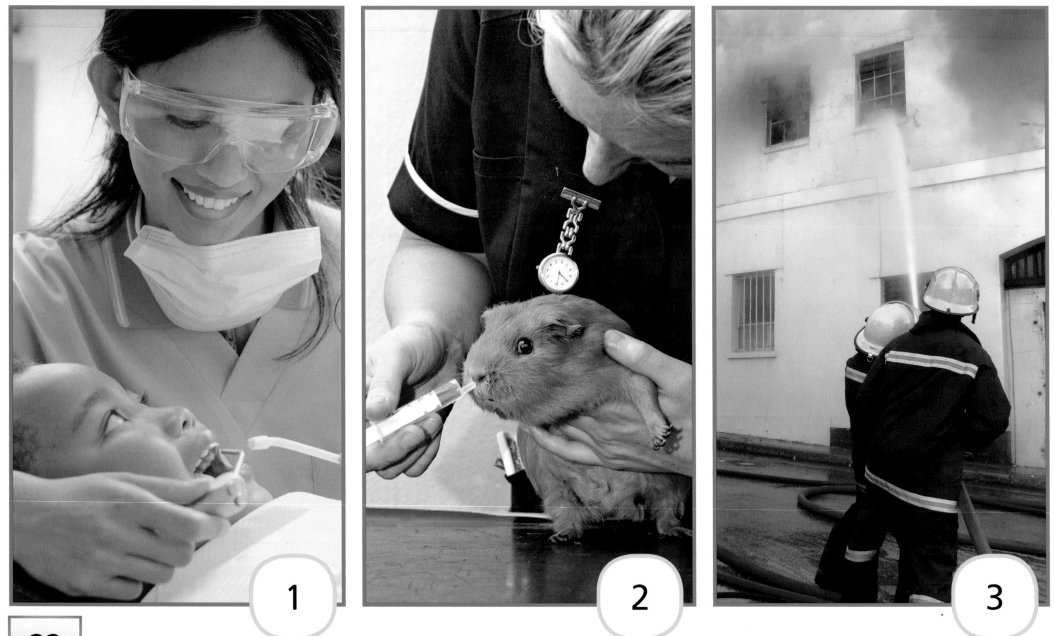

1

2

3

Answers on page 24.

Words to Know

arrest — to be held by the police

community — group of people with something in common. A community can be a group of people who live in the same area.

crime — something against the rules. People commit crimes when they break a law.

earn — to get something for work. People earn money for work.

fact — piece of information

goods — things that people eat or use. Food, toys, and clothing are goods.

paramedic — someone who helps transport people to see the doctor

patient — someone who is cared for at the hospital or dentist's office

services — jobs people do for each other. Serving food, cleaning a house, and driving a bus are services.

skill — the ability to do something. Riding a bike is a skill.

subject — something people study in school. Science is a subject.

Index

Note to Parents and Teachers

Before Reading:

Tell children that a community is a group of people. There are many different and similar communities around the world. Some communities are schools, families, neighborhoods, religious groups, and work places. Ask children to brainstorm a list of people who help the community. Create a chart of their ideas. As children are sharing their ideas, ask them why we need each person in our community.

After Reading:

• Divide children into different types of community workers: a person who helps us stay healthy, stay safe, helps others learn, and who helps animals. Ask them to make a list with their group about things their community worker does. Then they can make a skit and/or poster that describes their community worker. Children can make props, costumes, and pictures to aid their performance.

• Talk to the children about the job they would like to have when they are older. Children can write or draw a picture about the job they are interested in.

Answer to questions on page 22

Photo 1 shows a hygienist helping people to keep their teeth clean.
Photo 2 shows a vet caring for an animal.
Photo 3 shows firefighters putting out a fire.